THE ART OF

DAY TRADING

Unleash Your Potential and Master the Art of Day Trading

Maximize Your Profits, Minimize Your Risks: The Ultimate Guide to Day Trading Success..

WOOD ROBERT

—

Table of Contents

CHAPTER 1

Introduction to Day Trading

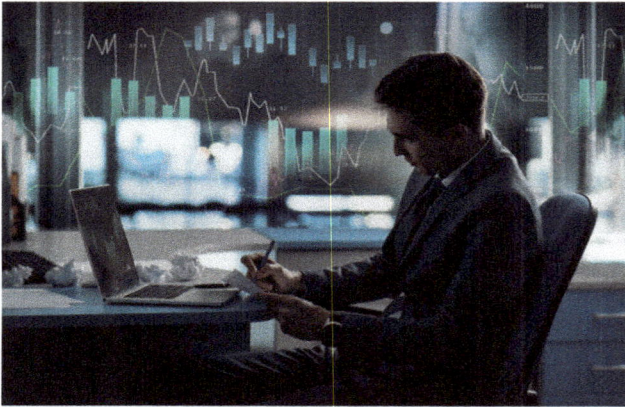

As in any commercial company, equipment is essential and day trade is no exception. Since you are in search of day trading equipment, I suppose you know perfectly well the server farms used by automated trading companies based in New York and Connecticut. Well, this is not an architectural document for the construction of the next data center; however, you will get all the basics of the equipment you will need to start day trading. Not only will you need a strong approach to day trading, but the day when the needs of its teams are just as important when setting up day trading.

Computers

Day trading sometimes involves taking advantage of very fast moves; sometimes, you will be in a trade for less than 10 seconds. You will need a day trading computer with a fast processor to manage the speed at which you need to run. I would recommend at least a Intel 10th gen with a minimum of 16GB of RAM and a 250GB hard drive.

One thing to consider is the usability of quad-core processors. five-core doesn't necessarily mean faster if the trading software doesn't support it.

Monitors

I work with four monitors to allow me to monitor various actions and other technical indicators simultaneously. It is a really personal preference; someday, traders avoid using a laptop, while others need 12 monitors to operate. If your day trading computer demands a multi-monitor setup, you will also need to acquire a video card that supports multi-monitor setup. I recommend researching and checking prices on eBay. That's where I bought all my video cards and got over 50% off the retail price.

You can also visit websites like digital tigers; even if you don't buy from them, you can get an idea of what you need. One last note on monitors, make sure you have monitors with good resolution and keep the brightness low so as not to tire your eyes. Set up the monitors correctly at first and you will literally avoid the headache of looking at the screen all day.

Internet connection

Finally, at least one cable modem connection will be required. Trading is fast and your data needs to be faster. Here are some of the golden rules for managing Internet connections:

- No trading in the library: Networks are not secure and often fail with the smallest technical support in sight.

- Not Starbucks: Go for your coffee, not to show everyone that you are an exceptional trader. You will receive more questions and comments than you can imagine.

- No 3G: 3G is meant for mobile phones and children who want to play angry birds. You are a professional trader and your connection speed must be greater than your child's age.

Data feed

Day trading will obviously require a real-time data source. You will need to acquire a real-time subscription from your broker. There will be a commission for most trades for which real-time data is required. Also, there will be an additional charge for viewing Tier 2 information. Live news will be slightly more expensive than the stock price data you are paying. It can be around $ 100 a month for an RT news source.

Backups

The worst that can happen is that your day trading computer can freeze it while trading. It is always important to have a laptop or backup computer that is configured with the appropriate trading software so that you can change the configuration quickly enough in the event of a hardware failure. It's important to have a backup for your day trading computer is having a backup Internet connection. I can't even count how many times my internet connection was cut during the trading session. This is a great risk and can cost a lot of money. If you are a serious trader, I suggest connecting your location with the ability to manage dual internet connections that can be changed on the fly in the event of a network outage with one of your providers. It's not worth being at risk for the small fees compared to having a backup.

Software

Software should be kept to a minimum with trading computers. You do not want system resources to be absorbed by third-party software not related to day trading. In addition to its trading software, I would suggest running antivirus and Microsoft Office software, but not much else.

Your day trading command center must be treated with the utmost respect and thought through carefully. The goal is to prevent your car from crashing once and the sales window to be lost in a leak at 9:30 a.m. Also, switching between multiple screens and windows will be too much for a laptop. So, don't go cheap. Spend money upfront for a chance at success.

CHAPTER 2:

Basics of Day Trading

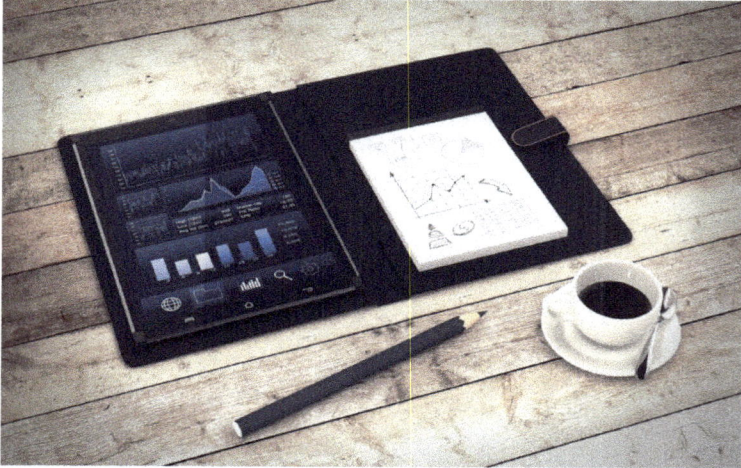

I t's time for you to look at the day trading process works. You could just blindly jump in, but that's a recipe for disaster. Instead, let's get you started on how to smartly engage in day trading.

The first question to ask yourself is, how big an investment are you planning on making in your day trading efforts? You need to consider not only how much money you're willing to invest, but also how much time. Many investors look at day trading as an escape from their normal jobs, others see it as an answer to the uncertainties of the job market. While you may hunger to day trade full time, people do succeed as part-time day traders while working a primary job. Beginners may also want to spend some time simulating investments to get a feel for how comfortable you are with the process and how much talent you may have. People who want to start Day Trading should do several things to put themselves on the right path. Firstly, they need to step back and ask themselves whether this form of trading is really for them. Day Trading is not for the faint of heart. It requires a high level of focus and is not something people should risk their retirement plan to do.

Actually, beginners should consider opening a practice account before committing their hard-earned money. Reputable brokerage firms provide such accounts or stock market simulators to aspiring traders, through which they can make hypothetical trades and see the results.

In addition, aspiring day traders need to have a suitable brokerage account before they begin trading. Some brokers charge high transaction costs, which can erode the gains from winning trades. In fact, good brokers provide research resources that are invaluable to traders.

Aspiring traders who discover that Day Trading is not for them should do what smart investors do, which is engaging in long-term investing in a diversified fund or stock portfolio. They should regularly add more funds to their accounts and let the magic of growth expand their investment portfolio. This may not be as thrilling as Day Trading, but it is better than doing something that will clean out one's savings.

Consider Constraints and Goals

Before investing the time, energy, and effort in learning or creating and then practicing Day Trading, prospective day traders should consider their constraints and goals. For example:

Traders need to determine whether they have enough capital to engage in Day Trading. If they lack the capital, they should wait until they have it while they are learning about and practicing different trading strategies.

They should understand that achieving consistent gains takes several months to a year, even when practicing several hours each day. For those who practice intermittently, it will take longer to achieve success; therefore, prospective traders should put in the time and effort required to achieve their goals.

Once they start trading, they need to commit to trading for at least two hours a day, depending on their commitments.

Until their trading profits match or surpass their income, new day traders should not quit their day jobs. They also need to determine the ideal time of day to trade based on their other commitments. In addition, they should ensure that their trading strategy fits that time of day. Essentially, their trading strategy needs to fit their life.

People who want to venture into Day Trading need to determine whether they want to do it with the aim of quitting their regular jobs. To get to the point where they can replace their day jobs by Day Trading, prospective traders need to understand that they will probably need to practice and trade for a year or more, depending on their dedication.

Aspiring day traders should consider the factors above before investing their time and money in learning this line of trade.

Choose a Broker

While new traders are practicing and developing their trading strategies, they should set aside some time to choose a good and reputable broker. It may be the same they opened a demo or practice account with, or it may be another one. Actually, choosing the right broker is one of the most important transactions day traders will make because they will entrust all of their capital.

Capital Needed to Start Day Trading

How much capital people need to start Day Trading depends on the market they trade, where they trade, and the style of trading they wish to do. There is a legal minimum capital requirement set by the stock market to day trade; however, based on the individual trading style, there is also a recommended minimum.

A day trader needs to have enough capital to have the flexibility to make a variety of trades and withstand a losing streak, which will inevitably happen. Traders also need to determine the amount of money they need, which requires them to address risk management. In addition, they should not risk more than 2% of their account on a single trade.

Capital is the most important component when it comes to Day Trading. By risking only 1% or 2%, even a long losing streak will keep most of the capital intact. For day traders in the United States, the legal minimum balance needed to day trade stocks is $25,000. Traders whose balance drops below this amount cannot engage in Day Trading until they make a deposit that brings their balance above $25,000.

To have a buffer, U.S. day traders should have at least $30,000 in their trading accounts. Stocks usually move in $0.01 increments and trade in lots of 100 shares; therefore, with at least $30,000 in their accounts, day traders will have some flexibility.

Day traders can usually get leverage up to four times the amount of their capital. A trader with $30,000 in his/her account, for example, can trade up to $120,000 worth of stock at any given time. Essentially, the trade price multiplied by the position size can equal more than the trader's account balance.

Day traders can trade fewer volatile stocks, which often require a bigger position size and a smaller stop loss, or stocks that are more volatile, with often require a smaller position size and a larger stop loss. Either way, the total risk on each trade should not be more than 2% of the trading account balance.

Infrastructure Concerns

While it may sound mundane, spending some time on your workspace and technology can be well worth it. Day trading can be stressful, so a work area that provides quiet and privacy can be helpful. Don't underestimate the importance of a reliable Internet connection and a backup method of controlling your investments in case your network goes down. These days it's not hard to have a fast land-based Internet connection while also having the ability to use your smartphone as a wireless hotspot if your main connection goes down. It only takes one network failure when you have a big investment on the line, to convince you of the importance of a backup Internet access plan.

Understanding the Market

It's one thing to say you want to invest in stocks. It's another thing to figure out what stocks you should be investing in. Investors break down the market into different sectors, such as "retailers," "manufacturers," "utilities," "airlines," "energy," "health care," and others. Day traders can choose to target all these sectors or choose to specialize in one or more. As a beginner, focusing on one sector may be advantageous, particularly if it's one you're already familiar with.

Since as a day trader, you're interested in identifying opportunities for small changes in stocks, not long-term growth. This means you'll need ample funding. U.S. based day traders need a minimum of $25,000 for their trading account, according to Securities and Exchange Commission (SEC) rules. This means you'd really need at least $30,000 to have some flexibility. Keep in mind; in the U.S., you can currently leverage your trading capital up to 400%. This means that you could control $120,000 worth of stock with your $30,000. As you learned earlier, this also means you could suffer four times the losses on your investments. Be aware too, that if you don't maintain your maintenance margin amount, you can receive a margin call. In planning for your trading account, it would be better to have more funds available, since that would make more stocks available for your consideration. Remember too, it's usually more cost efficient to buy shares in multiples of 100, meaning a small investment kitty will either limit you to cheaply priced stocks or buying stocks in smaller increments than are less cost-effective. If you can devote more funds to your trading account, you'll be able to pursue more opportunities, and have the wherewithal to recover from losses.

Calculating a Simple Moving Average

The moving average is a basic tool investor use to monitor a stock's behavior over a defined period. The investor simply adds the stock's closing price for a specific period (two weeks, a month, a quarter, etc.) and then divides that number by the number of trading days in that period. A trader will calculate a short-term moving average and a long-term moving average for a stock (Actually, you'll probably calculate a few more than this to get a better sense of the stock's behavior). A simple moving average can tell you whether a stock is on a rising or declining trend.

An important point for many traders is when the short term moving average rises above or below the long-term moving average. A short-term moving average that crosses above a long-term moving average often indicates the stock is about to begin an upward trend. The opposite is also true.

One approach to using moving averages compares a specific short-term moving average (50 days) with a specific long-term moving average (200 days). If the 50-day average moves below the 200-day average, you have a bearish signal. This is known as a "Death Cross." If the 50 average moves above the 200-day average, it is a bullish signal, and is known as a "Golden Cross." While it would be nice if you could rely solely on such a simple system, remember that relying only on a moving average approach is unreliable. It's better to use this information as another bit of information when making your trading plans.

CHAPTER 3:

Different Types of Trading

Trading in Stocks

The thought of trading in stocks scares away many investors. Individuals who have never traded are terrified by the fact that one can easily lose money with wrong decisions. The reality is stock trading is a risky activity. However, when approached with the right market knowledge, it is an efficient way of building your net worth.

So, what is a stock? A stock is a share. It is also termed as equity. Basically, it is a financial instrument which amounts to ownership in a particular company. When an individual purchases a stock or shares, it means that they own a portion or fraction of the company. For instance, say a trader owns 10,000 shares in a company with 100,000 shares. This would mean that the individual has 10% ownership of the stakes. The buyer of such shares is identified as a shareholder. Therefore, the more shares one owns, the larger the proportion of the company which they own. Every time the value of the company shares rise, your share value will also rise. Similarly, if the value falls, your share value also declines. When a company makes a profit, the shareholders are also bestowed with the profits in the form of dividends.

Preferred stock and common stock are the two main types of stocks you should be aware of. The difference that lies between these stocks is that with common stocks, it carries voting rights. This means that a shareholder has an influence on company meetings. Hence, they can have a say in company meetings where the board of directors is elected. On the other hand, preferred shares lack voting rights. However, they are identified as "preferred" shares or stocks because of their preference over common stocks. If a company goes through liquidation, shareholders with preferred shares will be preferred to receive assets or dividends.

Far from the information provided about the varying kinds of stock, a day trader doesn't necessarily have to understand the difference. Remember, you are only a day trader. Thus, you will only buy shares for a short period before selling them on the same day.

Basing on the factors pointed out above, the stock market could be evaluated as follows.

Capital Requirements

According to the Pattern Day Trader Rule, the minimum brokerage balance you are required to maintain for you to trade in stocks is at least $25,000. Without a doubt, this is a lot of money to start with. Surprisingly, there are tons of traders who began with a lower amount than that. To understand how this rule applies, you need to know what it means to be a pattern day trader. This is the type of trader whereby they execute more than four traders within five business days in their margin accounts.

Leverage

There are two ways of trading in stocks. You could either choose to trade using a margin account or a cash account. With the margin account, it gives a trader the opportunity of buying their stocks on margin. Conversely, with cash accounts, you only buy the stocks for the amount of money present in your account. In other words, you will be trading with a leverage ratio of 1:1.

The notion of trading on margin implies that you will be seeking for funds from your broker. This means that you will be able to buy more stocks far beyond what you can normally afford. To use a margin account, a trader will be required to have at least $2,000 as their starting capital. However, some brokers will demand more. Once your margin account is open, you can get a loan amounting to 50% of the buying price of the stock.

In a real-life example, say you make an initial deposit of $10,000 to your margin account. Since you deposited about 50% of the buying price, it means you are worth twice as much, i.e., $20,000. In other words, your buying power is worth twice what you deposited. Therefore, when you buy stocks worth $5,000, your buying power will reduce to $15,000. Your leverage ratio is therefore 1:2. Traders with a good trading relationship with their brokers could have this ratio increased to even 1:8.

Liquidity

With regard to liquidity, you can be certain that trading in stocks is not a bad idea. There are over 10,000 stocks present in the U.S. stock exchanges. Most of these stocks are traded daily. Dealing with these stocks guarantees that you evade the common issues of slippage or manipulation.

Volatility

A trader shouldn't worry about the volatility of the stock market as they often go through cycles of high and low. This is not a bad thing as a trader simply needs to study when the markets are rising and be wary of the instances when markets seem to fall.

Basing on these factors, it would be true to argue that stocks have got good volatility and liquidity. The only issue with stocks is that they have a high capital requirement.

Trading in Forex

Most traders would argue that trading in Forex is quite complicated. However, it's not. Just like any other form of trading, you have to stick to the basic rules. In this case, you need to buy when the market is rising and ensure you sell when the market is dropping. Basically, trading in forex involves the process of trading in currencies. In simpler terms, a trader exchange currency for others based on certain agreed rates. If you have traveled to foreign countries and exchanged your currency against their local currencies, then you should understand how trading in Forex works.

At first, it could seem confusing to choose the best currencies, but a trader should simply go for major currencies. Some of the frequently traded currencies include the U.S. dollar, Japanese Yen, European Union Euro, Australian dollar, Canadian dollar, and the Swiss franc. An important thing you ought to understand about Forex trading is that you need to trade in pairs. This means that when you are buying one currency, you should do this while simultaneously selling another. If you do some digging, you will notice that currencies are quoted in pairs, i.e. USD/JPY or EUR/USD. Below is an image showing how currencies are quoted in pairs.

EUR/USD
Base Currency   Quote Currency

Often, the most traded Forex products include:

- USD/JPY

- EUR/USD

- GBP/USD

An important thing to keep in mind with regards to Forex trading, is that the market is highly volatile. This means that a trader could easily lose a lot of money within a single day. Before venturing into this market, a trader should take the time to understand this market in detail.

The Forex market could be evaluated as follows.

Capital Requirements

With the number of brokers over the internet, it is relatively easy to begin Forex trading. The best part is that different brokers will require varying amounts of capital from you. Hence, you could settle for the best, depending on how much you can afford. You can trade in Forex with just $1,000 as your starting capital.

Leverage

Typically, leverage in the Forex market stands at 1:100. This implies that if you have $2,000 in your trading account, you can trade $200,000. The ratio varies depending on the forex trader you deal with. Some traders offer leverage of 1:200.

Liquidity

Liquidity is not an issue in the world of forex trading. The only problem is that a trader does not have access to real-time volume data simply because the market is decentralized.

Volatility

Considering the fact that there is high leverage in Forex trading, it implies that little movement in the market could earn one huge profit. The market's volatility is quite impressive, but not as volatile as the stock market.

Basing on these factors, trading in Forex is a smart move. A trader can begin trading with as little as $1,000. Also, with the high leverage present in this market, it is easy to earn huge returns with the right moves.

Trading in Futures

Today, most traders prefer to trade in futures due to their associated advantages. Trading in futures is quite flexible and diverse. The good news is that a trader can employ almost any methodology to trade. Some traders shy away from this form of trading due to their limited knowledge about futures. Also, others are discouraged from trading futures because they think that it is difficult. Well, to some extent, this is true. Comparing trading in futures to trading in stocks, the former is very risky. There are different forms of futures contracts, including currencies, energies, interest rates, metals, food sector futures, and agricultural futures. The best futures contracts you will find in the market are briefly discussed in the following lines.

S&P 500 E-mini

Most traders will fancy the idea of trading in the S&P 500 E-mini because of its high liquidity aspect. It also appeals to most investors because of its low day trading margins. You can conveniently trade in S&P 500 E-mini around the clock, not to mention that you will also benefit from its technical analysis aspect. Essentially, the S&P 500 E-mini is a friendly contract since you can easily predict its price patterns.

10 Year T-Notes

10 Year T-Notes are also ranked as one of the best contracts to trade in. Considering its sweet maturity aspect, most traders would not hesitate to trade in this futures contract. There are low margin requirements that a trader will have to meet when trading in 10 Year T-Notes.

Crude Oil

Crude oil also stands as one of the most popular commodities in futures trading. It is an exciting market because of its high daily trading volume of about 800k. Its high volatility also makes the market highly lucrative.

Gold

This is yet another notable futures contract. It might be expensive to trade in gold; however, it is a great hedging choice more so in poor market conditions.

Capital Requirements

The amount of money required to begin trading in futures will vary. Some brokers will require a trader to have about $5,000. However, there are those who would require only $2,000. It is vital for a trader to choose the best broker who is flexible enough to allow them to trade with the little capital they have.

Leverage

Leverage will also vary depending on the type of futures you trade-in. The contract value will also have an impact on the amount of leverage that you will have.

Liquidity

Just like leverage, the liquidity aspects of futures will also depend on the futures you are trading. Accordingly, it is important for any trader to regularly check the respective volumes of contracts before trading with them.

Volatility

Futures are volatile. The advantage gained by using high leverage ensures that a trader makes good profit with little price changes in the market.

CHAPTER 4:

The Mindset of a Trader

We will talk about what you should be doing, to make sure that you are not failing in your endeavors to start your options trading journey without making it too hard on yourself. In this chapter, we will show you what you could be doing to make options trading your lifestyle and to not only help you to start your trading journey but to stay on track. These daily patterns will help you not to fail when trading, and we understand that you might fail a couple of times in anything you do, and it is understandable to do so. Nonetheless, this chapter will show you how to make sure you are consistent and not failing. Many successful people have followed these habits, to get optimal results in all of their aspects of life, whether it be job-related or anything else. Make sure you start implementing all of these habits after you are done reading this book as it will help you to make options trading much easier for you. The reason why this chapter might sound philosophical is that the only way you will see success with options trading is if you do it consistently. For you to do that, you need to change your current lifestyle by being more productive and disciplined. You have to remember, being successful in options trading is more of a lifestyle.

Plan your Day Ahead

Planning your day ahead of time is crucial, not only does planning out your day help you be more prepared for your day moving forward, but it will also help you to become more aware of the things you shouldn't be doing, hence wasting your time.

Moreover, planning your day will truly help you with making the most out of your time, that being said, we will talk about two things. First, benefits of planning out your day and second, how to go about planning out your day. So, without further ado, let us dive into the benefits of planning out your day.

It will help you prioritize

Yes, planning out your day will help you prioritize a lot of things in your day to day life. You can allow time limits to the things you want to work on the most to least, for example, if you're going to write your book and you are super serious about it. Then you need a specific time limit every day in which you work on a task wholeheartedly without any worries of other things until the time is up. Then you move on to the next job in line, so when you schedule out your whole day, and you give yourself time limits, then you can prioritize your entire day. The same thing goes for your trading, make sure you allocate time for trading, which will allow you to be more focused on your research, hence making you more successful.

Summarize your normal day

Now, before we start getting into planning out your whole day ahead, you need to realize that to plan your entire day, you need to know precisely what you are doing that day. Which means you need to write down every single thing you do on a typical day and write down the time you start and end, it needs to be detailed in terms of how long take for your transportation to get to work, etc.

Now after you have figured out your whole day, you can decide how to prioritize your day moving on could be cutting out a task that you don't require or shortening your time for a job that doesn't need that much time. After you have your priorities for the day, you can add pleasurable tasks into your day like hanging out with your friends, etc.

Arrange your day

It is crucial that you arrange your day correctly, so the best way to organize your day is to make sure you get all your essential stuff done earlier in the day when your mind is fresh. After that's done, you can have some time for yourself to relax and do whatever it is that you want. But make sure you get all the things that need to be done before you can move on to free time for yourself. Another thing that will help you is to set time limits on each task, and once you start setting time limits, you will be more likely to get the job done.

Remove all the fluff

So, what I mean by that is remove all the things that are holding you back from achieving your goals. Make sure you remove all of the things that are holding you back from getting the things that you need to be doing. If you have time for the fluff, do it if not, then work on your priorities first. In conclusion, planning out your day will help you tremendously! Make sure you plan out your day every day to ensure successful and accomplished days.

Cut out negative people

This task might be the hardest to do, but it is quite essential, see the people who you are around are the people who will create your personality. So if you are around negative people, you will develop adverse circumstances for yourself, so if you are around people who are not upbeat about life and find everything wrong and never see the good in anyone, you need to cut them out and be around people who are happy and ready for what life has to offer. Now I get it, some cynical people can be your family members, and you can't cut them out, the ideal thing to do is 1. Make them understand what they are doing wrong 2. Show them how they can change their life. And if they still want to remain the same, then keep your distance.

In conclusion, it is essential that you are in a grateful "vibe" as it will not only help you with your mental and physical health, but it will also help you attract better people and better circumstances. Don't forget to practice the three methods we discussed for you to be in a grateful 'vibe" throughout the day and life! So be thankful!

Now that you have covered the part of being grateful, and how it can help you with your day to day life and eating habits. Let us give you some concrete ideas on how to change the way you live your experience and to make it better.

Stop Multitasking

I think we are all guilty of this at a time, and if we are multitasking right now, I need you to stop. Now multitasking could be a lot of things, and it could be as small as cooking and texting at the same time, or it could be as big as working on two projects at the same time. Studies are showing how multitasking can reduce your quality of work, which something you don't want to do if your goal is to get the best result out of the thing that you are doing. That being said, there are a lot more reasons as to why you shouldn't be multitasking, so without further ado, let's get into the primary reasons why multitasking can be harmful.

You're Not As Productive

Believe it or not, you tend to be a lot less productive when you are multitasking. When you go from one project to another or anything else for that matter, you don't put all your effort into your work. You are always worried about the project that you will be moving into next. So moving back and forth from one project to another will affect your productivity if you want to get the most out of your work you need to be focused on one thing at a time and make sure you get it done to the best of your abilities. Plus, you are more likely to make mistakes, which will not help you work to the best of your ability.

You Become Slower at your Work

When you are multitasking, chances are you will end up being slower at completing your projects. You would be in a better position if you were to focus on one project at a time instead of going back and forth, which of course, helps you complete them faster. So, the thing that enables you to be faster at your projects when you're not multitasking is the mindset, we often don't realize how much mindset comes into play. When you are going back and forth from one project to another, you are in a different mental state going into another project, which takes time to build and break. So by the time you have managed to get into the mindset of project A, you are already moving into project B, it is always best that you devote your time and energy one project at a time if you want it to doe did an at a faster pace.

Set yourself a Goal (Time, Quality, etc)

All in all, multitasking will do you no good. It will only make you slower at your work and make you less productive. Making sure you stop multitasking is essential, as it will only help you live a better life. One thing to remember from this chapter is to put all your energy at one thing at a time, and this will yield you a lot better projects or anything that you are working towards to be great. If you want to be more successful and live a better life, you need to make sure your projects are quality as I can't stress this point enough. You are probably reading this book because you want to get better at living your life or achieve goals which you haven't yet. One of the reasons why you are not living the life that you want or haven't reached your goal could be a lot of things but, one of the items could be the quality of your work, which could be taking a hit because of your multitasking. So, review yourself, and find out why you haven't achieved your goal and why you are not living the life that you want.

Then if you happen to stumble upon multitasking being the limiting factor or the quality of your work, I want you to stop multitasking and start working on one project at a time while giving it your full attention. What you will notice is that your work will have a higher quality and will be completed in a quicker amount of time following the steps listed above, which will change your life and help you achieve your life goals in a better more efficient way.

Now that we have talked about some action items in regard to

---

making options trading more of a lifestyle by changing the way you set up your day. Let us talk about some of the lifestyle changes you need to make in regard to making trading more easily for you.

CHAPTER 5:

Trading is not Gambling

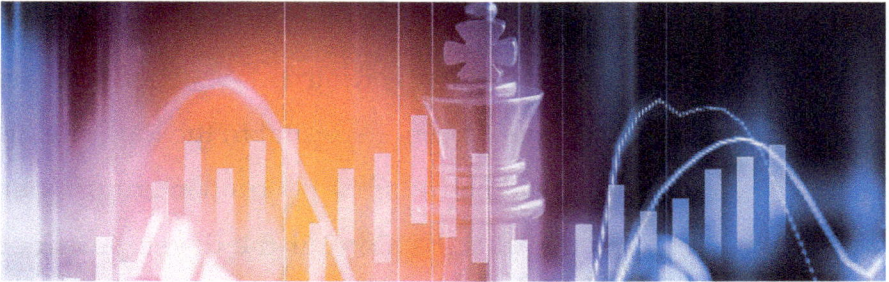

D ay trading usually attracts people with strong impulses such as gamblers and other people who feel that they are entitled to win. Avoid these mindsets. Stop behaving like an irresponsible teenager.

You must begin developing the discipline of a master.

Masters think, feel, and act differently than average people. Try to look within yourself and eliminate your illusions. Change your old methods of acting, thinking, and being.

It can be extremely difficult to change, but if you really want to be a profitable day trader, you need to work on changing and improving yourself. In order to succeed, you need the right form of motivation, know-how, and discipline.

The downside to such delays is often a faulty sense of size estimation in taking your trading position. Hence, the resulting increased exposure to financial risk you become disadvantaged by. Beware of your procrastination when it comes to productive openings that are currently available in Day Trading. If you possess this tendency, consider getting rid of it as soon as possible before it costs you a lot more capital in the long run. In case you are not prone to the frequent postponement of your responsibilities to a later date, be alert for the development of this mentality with the trading company that you keep. You can quickly become influenced by the kind of traders from whom you seek advice on more complex trading strategies. When present, stockbrokers affect your trading ethos, as well.

Poor trading etiquette from these external sources will rub off on you and vice versa. Try to keep the company of well-known responsible trading partners and stockbrokers when the need arises. Another rationalization scenario involves a run of profitable results. Based on a series of trade deals that made you successive returns, you begin to convince your brain of your seemingly high intelligence. This false belief in your skills may lead you to overestimate your trading expertise. Before long, you may start engaging in Day Trading on a hunch rather than apply logic to your decisions. You stop referring to your trusted trading plan and jump into many trading opportunities haphazardly. After a while, these instances of carelessness and trading arrogance will catch up with you because they always inevitably do. Your chances of plunging into a financial disaster go up.

With your eventual financial ruin come the cases of psychological meltdown leading to a negative feedback loop. A wrong decision from your misplaced sense of conceitedness will invariably lead to high-risk exposure. As a result, you suffer significant losses eventually, and consequently, your emotional health suffers, causing you to spiral into a state of depression. This loop is often self-propagating, meaning that it feeds onto itself. Bad decisions lead to adverse outcomes and a fragile mindset, which, in turn, is prone to make more bad decisions, and the loop goes on and on. Keep in mind that in Day Trading, such a feedback loop is often disastrous. All these adverse effects arise from your initial false sense of justification for a wrong deed.

Beware of your Trading Decisions

This advice is so apparent that it sounds redundant when mentioned. However, decisions are typically the product of your reasoning and judgment at a particular moment. When it comes to decisions on Day Trading, psychological influence is often a determining factor in the process. Keeping your wits about you is very crucial, especially when everything seems to be out of control. You need to realize that every trade has its ups and downs and how you deal with the challenging times are often more consequential. Try to maintain a logical mindset when making Day Trading choices from a variety of bad options. When it seems that an imminent financial downturn is inevitable, the extent of your loss becomes essential. In this case, you will need to make a sensible decision on the degree of losing margins that you can tolerate adequately.

At this point, you are probably in a state of so many overwhelming emotions that your foggy mental faculties become clouded. An expected human response is to run away from danger, naturally, but in certain situations, fleeing may not be an option. A reflex in a trading scenario often leads to an impulsive decision. Such a choice is, in turn, typically not well thought or deliberative. You should confront your unfavorable circumstances head-on and attempt to fix the situation; however, hopeless. This sense of perseverance is usually the essence of most trading excursions, especially when the times become financially rough. Going through the loss of some capital and other Day Trading challenges is often a painful experience that can lead to illogical decisions.

Always remember to uphold vigilance and adhere strictly to the guidelines in your trading plan when confronted with obstacles during your trades. The trading plan usually has instructions on how to handle these seemingly desperate situations. In addition, the prior preparation of any trading guide is generally free of emotional or psychological influence; hence, you can rely on it to maintain neutrality. Also, beware of making trading resolutions when going through a phase with a foul mood. Such conclusions are bound to lead you into a financial catastrophe, especially if you are not careful. Learn to put off the verdict to a time when you can resume logical thinking. When you make any rash decision, it can only result in your further exposure to even more risk.

Keep Your Emotions in Check

Learn to stick to a Day Trading system and method that you trust. Such a strategy may be one that has a history of always making significant returns. Once you master and fully grasp how to apply a specific approach to your trading deals, try to fine-tune it to your preference based on your ultimate objectives. Afterward, stick to this tried, practiced, and tested system in all your searches for valid trade deals. On some days, the stock market may be slow with a low volume of trade. The volatility in such a case is often negligible. However, due to an unchecked emotional influence, you develop a sense of greed or lust for profits.

The desire for benefits on a slow day is common. It leads to the urge to trade on anything to make a small profit. In this situation, you will move from Day Trading into gambling. Trading requires a logical mindset on your part with a lack of psychological attachment whatsoever. Gambling is a consequence of emotional and mental factors running amok in your Day Trading system. If a particular trading style worked on multiple times in the past, teach your brain to consider it. Your trusted trading system will indicate a lack of valid trade opportunities on a specific slow market day. In this case, curb your emotions, desires, and urges to chase a quick profit; however strong they seem.

You should never allow yourself to resort to gambling under any circumstances. Gambling is detrimental to healthy and responsible Day Trading behavior. The risk exposure exponentially rises when you grow accustomed to the desire for profits. If a given day of trading is unfavorable, you should not take part in invalid and unworthy deals. In addition, you should only trade on verifiable opportunities. At certain times, you may experience a series of successive returns in a relatively short period. Learn to know when to stop and how to curb your lust for wanting more returns. Trust your system to trade only on valid deals; however, multiple opportunities are available. An emotion that goes unmonitored in such situations is the greed for more profit.

You convince yourself psychologically that the various deals could be a sign of your lucky day. This mentality in a false belief is wrong, and you need to be aware of it. Your psychology can play deceitful tricks on your logical mind leading to high-risk trading deals. You must realize that in Day Trading, it is almost impossible to get more returns out of a system than what the stock market offers. Emotional corruption also comes into play in a scenario where you bite off more than you can chew.

The greed for substantial amounts of returns may cause you to take high-risk trading positions for a chance at quick profits. However, you must remember that profits and losses are both possible outcomes from a Day Trading session. Therefore, you need to learn to trade in amounts that you can afford to lose. After all, Day Trading involves taking a chance based on a speculative position. You should practice trading in small amounts of money within the confines of low-risk deals. In this case, a potential loss may not be as damaging as the earlier high-risk trading position driven by greed. Eliminate the role of emotions in Day Trading and learn to accept the uncertainty of an unknown future outcome.

Be Patient When Trading

Patience is a crucial trait to have when you take part in Day Trading due to the upswings and downward trends in stock prices. It can become challenging to identify the right entry or exit point for a particular trading opportunity, given the fluctuating nature of a volatile market. However, when you master the art of being patient and studying the trade intently, you can come up with a winning strategy. Having a planned approach is essential, and you should prepare one before engaging in any Day Trading. Often, most seasoned traders include trading strategies for different market conditions in their trading plans. Hence, when making your trading plan, consider incorporating a trading strategy within it.

If unsure of how to proceed, you can always seek the assistance of qualified stockbrokers. They have the experience of encountering various Day Trading scenarios in the real world. If trustworthy, they could provide you with invaluable insights on coming up with a proper strategy. Now it is up to you to stick to the plan in every session in which you participate. Patience demands that you pay attention to the planned strategy and ignore any attractive distractions when trading. For instance, a brief upswing from a potential price action breakout may be misleading. It might cause you to falsely believe that the stock price is about to pick momentum and keep rising on the chart.

However, as attractive as this scenario might be, a sense of diligent patience demands that you ignore it and refer to your strategy. Upon referral to your trading plan strategy, you may encounter the concept of false breakouts. You also learn that these false upswings in trend usually follow a prolonged period of price consolidated. As a result, your patience allows you to evade a potentially wrong entry point to a trading position. You are also able to pick the right exit point from a particular trading session based on strategic patience. The price action chart acts merely as a guide for your trading actions and not the determining factor.

CHAPTER 6

Start Day Trading as a Business

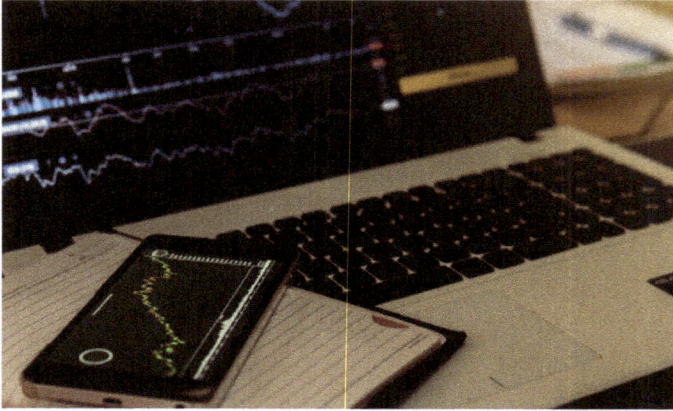

D ay trading can sound exciting, and it certainly is. And if you have larger amounts of capital to invest, and you're very good at it, then day trading can help you make large amounts of money over short time periods. But if you are just getting started, how much can you really earn day trading? Let's try looking at some realistic scenarios before having visions of millions of dollars.

The first thing to consider when you are trying to gauge the potential for success in any endeavor is the Pareto principle. Basically, this principle tells us that 20% of the people get 80% of the spoils. It doesn't matter what you're talking about, you could be talking about farmers. In that case, 20% of the farmers will be responsible for 80% of the output. In the case of the stock market, 20% of the investors will take 80% of the returns, and this most certainly applies to day trading. Most day traders are going to have to keep their day job, and many may end up losing their initial capital investment.

This isn't too out and out discouraging anyone from taking up day trading. There are many factors that will decide success or failure. For example, many people start off with high levels of excitement when taking on something new like day trading, but then they fizzle out very quickly. In short, they simply fail to put in the work required to excel. There could be a million reasons for it. Some people might wilt at the first sign of a challenge. Others may become bored with it. Some people are downright lazy – day trading actually takes work and they were hoping for a get rich quick scheme.

Just like only a small percentage of basketball players are ever going to be NBA stars, only a tiny percentage of day traders are going to rise to become the cream of the crop and make millions of dollars. That said, you can take action to seriously tip the odds in your favor. After all, many people practice basketball with an all-out effort and become top-level players, even if they aren't Kobe Bryant or Lebron James, they still may be very successful. The same principle applies to day trading. You may be a budding star or not – but if you dive in 100% to study the markets and finance and trading – you will up your odds significantly and even if you don't become a star, if you are a smart trader who hedges risk well then you may be able to make a solidly upper-middle-class income from it even if you don't become a top-level trader.

One rule is that disciplined traders, at least in the long run, are going to make more money than people who are flying by the seat of their pants kinds of people. The more capital you start with, the more money that you're going to make. But let's have a look at the minimum. Suppose that you start out with the recommended minimum amount of capital, which is $30,000.

Using leverage at 4:1, which means you can potentially control $120,000 worth of stock. Remember that there is a 1% rule on risk per trade and starting with $30,000 that means you'll be trading $300 at a time. Assuming you're a disciplined trader, you will have a good stop-loss strategy. Standard values are a win rate of 50% (that is half your trades are profitable) and your winners are around 1.5 times bigger than your losers. These numbers sound like no big deal, but it may take you a couple of years to get to this level. Now let's use these assumptions together with a guess that you make, on average, five trades per day or about 100 per month. With a 50% success rate, you'll have 50 profitable trades per month. A reasonable stop loss is $0.10, so with a 1.5 times ratio of the winner to loser, you're making $0.15 per share in profits. You can control 3,000 shares per trade. So that gives you a monthly profit of $22,500. Your losses come from the stop loss figure of ten cents a share, so you're going to lose $15,000 per month.

Your gross income will then be the difference, or $7,500 a month. However, remember that you'll need to pay lots of commissions. Brokers don't let you trade stock for free. In the end, your actual profit will probably be about $5,000 a month. Now, this isn't bad to get started. So, you're able to work from home, doing something fun and exciting that is even a little bit risky, and make an OK middle-class income from it. But it's probably not the kind of income you were hoping to see.

That isn't to say that you can't grow your business over time and make huge amounts of money. You absolutely can do that. However, what we're really trying to show here is that day trading really isn't a get rich quick scheme. It's not really different from any other kind of business that takes time, work, and energy to grow.

Of course, you might be better than average. If you are really good, maybe 65% of your trades turn out profitable and you're banking $8,000-$9,000 per month depending on the size of commissions you have to pay. That's not an unrealistic possibility; however, remember that not everyone is as talented as anyone else. Some people are going to do worse than the 50% success rate that we initially started with, and in those cases, they will make less money, maybe a couple thousand a month or less. Still, more won't make anything, and some are going to end up with losses.

The point of this discussion isn't to discourage people, it's to get you going into this with your eyes wide open and having realistic expectations. There is no doubt a few people reading this who will master day trading and end up millionaires. We sincerely hope that you are that one person!

CHAPTER 7:

All Tools of Trade

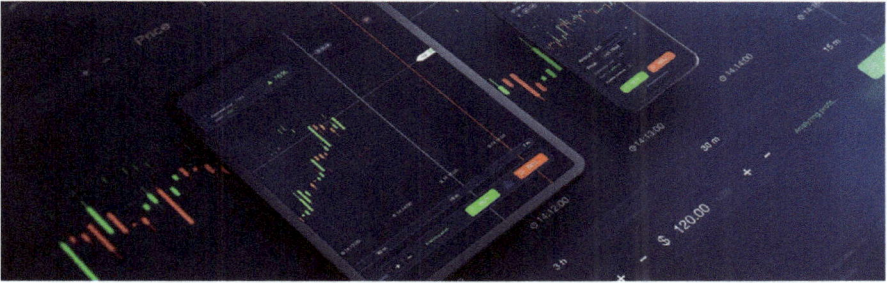

F or you to carry out day trading successfully, there are several tools that you need. Some of these tools are freely available, while others must be purchased. Modern trading is not like the traditional version. This means that you need to get online to access day trading opportunities.

Therefore, the number one tool you need is a laptop or computer with an internet connection. The computer you use must have enough memory for it to process your requests fast enough. If your computer keeps crashing or stalling all the time, you will miss out on some lucrative opportunities. There are trading platforms that need a lot of memory to work, and you must always put this into consideration.

Your internet connection must also be fast enough. This will ensure that your trading platform loads in real-time. Ensure that you get an internet speed that processes data instantaneously to avoid experiencing any data lag. Due to some outages that occur with most internet providers, you may also need to invest in a backup internet device such as a smartphone hotspot or modem. Other essential tools and services that you need include:

Brokerage

To succeed in day trading, you need the services of a brokerage firm. The work of the firm is to conduct your trades. Some brokers are experienced in day trading than others. You must ensure that you get the right day trading broker who can help you make more profit from your transactions. Since day trading entails several trades per day, you need a broker that offers lower commission rates. You also need one that provides the best software for your transactions. If you prefer using specific trading software for your deals, then look for a broker that allows you to use this software.

Real-time Market Information

Market news and data are essential when it comes to day trading. They provide you with the latest updates on current and anticipated price changes on the market. This information allows you to customize your strategies accordingly. Professional day traders always spend a lot of money seeking this kind of information on news platforms, in online forums or through any other reliable channels.

Financial data is often generated from price movements of specific stocks and commodities. Most brokers have this information. However, you will need to specify the kind of data you need for your trades. The type of data to get depends on the type of stocks you wish to trade.

Monitors

Most computers have a capability that enables them to connect to more than one monitor. Due to the nature of the day trading business, you need to track market trends, study indicators, follow financial news items, and monitor price performance at the same time. For this to be possible, you need to have more than one processor so that the above tasks can run concurrently.

Classes

Although you can engage in day trading without attending any school, you must get trained on some of the strategies you need to succeed in the business. For instance, you may decide to enroll for an online course to acquire the necessary knowledge in the business. You may have all the essential tools in your possession, but if you do not have the right experience, all your efforts may go to waste.

Day Trading Pricing Charts

Charts are used by traders to monitor price changes. These changes determine when to enter or exit a trading position. There are several charts used in day trading. Although these charts differ in terms of functionality and layout, they typically offer the same information to day traders.

Some of the most common day trading charts includes:

1. Line charts

2. Bar charts

3. Candlestick charts

For each of the above charts, you must understand how they work as well as the advantages/ disadvantages involved.

Line Charts

These are very popular in all kinds of stock trading. They do not give the opening price, just the closing price. You are expected to specify the trading period for the chart to display the closing price for that period. The chart creates a line that connects closing prices for different periods using a line.

Most day traders use this chart to establish how the price of a security has performed over different periods. However, you cannot rely on this chart as the only information provider when it comes to making some critical trading decisions. This is because the chart only gives you the closing price. This means that you may not be able to establish other vital factors that have contributed to the current changes in the price.

Bar Charts

These are lines used to indicate price ranges for a particular stock over time. Bar charts comprise vertical and horizontal lines. The horizontal lines often represent the opening and closing costs. When the closing price is higher than the opening price, the horizontal line is always black. When the opening price is higher, the line becomes red.

Bar charts offer more information than line charts. They indicate opening prices, highest and lowest prices as well as the closing prices. They are always easy to read and interpret. Each bar represents right information. The vertical lines indicate the highest and lowest prices attained by a particular stock. The opening price of a stock is always shown using a small horizontal line on the left of each vertical line. The closing price is a small horizontal line on the right.

Interpreting bar charts is not as easy as interpreting line charts. When the vertical lines are long, it shows that there is a significant difference between the highest price attained by a security and the lowest price. Large vertical lines, therefore, indicate that the commodity is highly volatile while small lines indicate slight price changes. When the closing price is far much higher than the opening price, it means that the buyers were more during the stated period. This indicates the likelihood of more purchases in the future. If the closing price is slightly higher than the purchase price, then very little purchasing took place during the period. Bar chart information is always differentiated using color codes.

Tick charts

Tick charts are not common in day trading. However, some traders use these charts for various purposes. Each bar on the chart represents numerous transactions. For instance, a 415 chart generates a bar for a group of 415 trade positions. One great advantage of tick charts is that they enable traders to enter and exit multiple positions quickly. This is what makes the charts ideal for day traders who transact volumes of stock each day.

These charts work by completing several trades before displaying a new bar. Unlike other charts, these charts work depending on the activity of each transaction, not on time. You can use them if you need to make faster decisions in your trade. Another advantage of tick chart is that you can customize each chart to suit your trading needs. You can apply the chart to diverse transaction sizes. The larger, the size, the higher the potential of making a profit from the trade.

Candlestick Charts

Candlestick charts are used on almost every trading platform. These charts carry a lot of information about the stock market and stock prices. They help you to get information about the opening, closing, highest, and lowest stock prices on the market. The opening price is always indicated as the first bar on the left of the chart, and the closing price is on the far right of the chart. Besides these prices, the candlestick chart also contains the body and wick. These are the features that differentiate the candlestick for other day trading charts.

One great advantage of candlestick charts entails the use of different visual aspects when indicating the closing, opening, highest, and lowest stock prices. These charts compute stock prices across different time frames. Each chart consists of three segments:

- The upper shadow

- The body

- The lower shadow

The body of the chart is often red or green color. Each candlestick is an illustration of time. The data in the candlestick represents the number of trades completed within the specified time. For instance, a 10-minute candlestick indicates 10 minutes of trading. Each candlestick has four points, and each point represents a price. The high point represents the highest stock price while low stands for the lowest price of a stock. When the closing price is lower than the opening price, the body of the candlestick will be red in color. When the closing price is higher, the body will be colored green.

Charting Software

Each of the above charts is created and viewed using specific software. This can be found in a brokerage firm, although you may also purchase this online depending on the type you want to use.

The software helps you identify the right opportunities by indicating when and how you should start and close positions. They always display the necessary patterns required to estimate future changes in stock prices. Using stock patterns, you can also establish continuations as well as reversals in the stock prices.

Chart software is available in many forms. You may find those that are in the form of mobile apps or others that are web-based. Getting the right software enables you to generate correct charts. This explains why you also need to incorporate technical analysis in your trades.

Most day trading chart tools are available free of charge. Some have a forum where you can learn from experienced traders as you use them. They also come with demo accounts that enable you to master day trading techniques before investing your capital in the business.

CHAPTER 8:

Day Trading Patterns

C harts and patterns are very important visual measures in day trading. They entail progress and updates of each, and everyday trade and traders use it to determine whether it is going to be a win or a loss during their activities. They are also a tool to predict future trading activities.

Below Are some of the Charts and Patterns that Are Used in Day Trading:

- Line chart.

The use of Line charts is one of the most famous types of charts in use. They only show the closing price for that period.

A continuous line will be drawn from a single closing price to the next immediate closing price. A line chart usually assists in bringing forth important information and making it easier to notice previous price points. However, it is inadvisable to base your principal determiners' online chart's data as it lacks crucial information.

- Use of bar charts.

These charts are made up of two kinds of lines: vertical and horizontal lines. Vertical lines will reflect the price range under a given period of time, whereas the horizontal lines cover prices on opening and closing. In certain cases where the opening price ends up being lower than the closing price, the produced line will usually be black and/ or red, for vice versa. Bar charts are believed to be an expression towards line charts, and they offer reliable and accurate information during reading and interpretation as compared to line charts.

Bar charts are much detailed, with plenty of information and therefore, so easy to read and interpret and preferred by most traders.

Bar charts are composed of open feet as they face to the left, vertical line and a closing foot produced that directs to the right. Every bar will have its high, open, low and close prices that happened during a specified interval that is normally defined by a trader. For instance, taking a trader that is opting for a two minutes interval bar chart(other measures than time still exist, like number of transactions called tick charts), then a new bar will be established after every two minutes, showing the open, high, low and close price for each and every minute of the interval used specified. Bar charts are responsible for indications of both the upward and downward movement where the price moved and the manner in which it moved during the bar establishment.

Below Are some of the Keywords that you Are Required to Comprehend from the Bar Charts:

- Open - This is the foremost price traded on the bar establishment and is indicated by a horizontal foot of a chart.
- High - The highest price possible traded during the specified interval assigned to the bar and is usually indicated by the top of the vertical bar.
- Low -Low keyword is the least price traded during the observed interval time for the bar and is usually indicated by the bottom of the produced vertical bar.

- Close - Close is usually the last price used for trading during the selected interval bar and is most commonly depicted on the chart by the horizontal foot on the right side of the bar.
- Range - the range is obtained by subtracting the top value from the bottom value of a chart's vertical bar. Range of bar = high – low.
- Direction - The direction the price moves during the bar is indicated by the location of the opening to that of the closing foot. A situation where the closing foot is bigger compared to opening foot, then definitely the price made an upward progression during the bar and on the other hand.
- Candlestick charts.

A candlestick is made up of three divisions namely, the body, higher shadow, and the lower shadow. The body is definitive from its green or red color. Every candlestick is a representation of a segmented period of time. The candlestick's related data will basically summarize all executed trades during that interval period of a specified time. A candlestick will have four data points namely, the open, high, low, and close.

Below Are some of the Keywords Common in Candlestick Charts:

- We have the high being represented by a straight line to a tail, wick or a shadow from the top of the body. The low of the candle is defined as the tailor lower shadow, represented by a

---

vertical line extending down from the body. When we have our close being higher than the open, then the body will eventually be colored green that symbolizes net price gain. When our open is reflecting higher than the close, then the body eventually will be colored red as it signifies a net price decline.

Candlestick Tends to Present Much of Emotion as Seen by the Wide Use of Colors:

- Hammer candlestick.

This is a type of candlestick that normally takes place when market security drops significantly than its opening price but however struggles to close near the opening price. It is normally in the shape of a hammer where the shadow is double the size of the real body.

Some of the Important Things to Point Out:

- A hammer is normally a recollection against the trend.
- It does not show you the movement of the trend.
- The background of the market is more essential than the hammer.

- Shooting star candlestick.

In technical analysis, the shooting star pin bar is composed of a single candlestick.

The bearish shooting star is more powerful because of its higher opening price as compared to the closing price.

- Bullish engulfing candlestick.

A bullish is just a confirmation of how the participants in the market agree on at that particular season.

- Single bar pattern.

This type of bar pattern represents a single trading day. A single bar pattern represents price activities within a given period of time. As a result, traders and investors use this chart type to spot trends and patterns.

CHAPTER 9:

Technical Analysis - How to

Analyze

This method focuses on studying the supply and demand of a market. The price will be seen to rise when the investor realizes the market is undervalued, and this leads to buying. If they think that the market is overvalued, the prices will start falling, and this is deemed the perfect time to sell.

You need to understand the movement of the various indicators to make the perfect decision. This method works on the premise that history usually repeats itself – a huge change in the prices affects the investors in any situation.

The Significance of Trends in Option Trading

Technical analysis works on the premise of the trend. These trends come by due to the interaction of the buyer and the seller. The aggressiveness of one of the parties in the market will determine how steep the trend becomes. To make a profit, you have to take advantage of the changes in the price movement.

To understand the direction of the trend, you ought to look at the troughs and peaks and how they relate to each other.

When looking for money in options trading, you ought to trade with a trend. The trend is what determines the decision you make when faced with a situation – whether to buy or to sell. You need to know the various signs that a prevailing trend is soon ending so that you can manage the risks and exit the trades the right way.

Characteristics of Technical Analysis

This analysis makes use of models and trading rules using different price and volume changes. These include the volume, price, and other different market info.

Technical analysis is applied among financial professionals and traders and is used by many option traders.

Prices Determine Trends

Technical analysts know that the price in the market determines the trend of the market. The trend can be up, down, or move sideways.

History Usually Repeats Itself

Analysts believe that an investor repeats the behavior of the people that traded before them. The investor sentiment usually repeats itself. Due to the fact that the behavior repeats itself, traders know that using a price pattern can lead to predictions. The investor uses the research to determine if the trend will continue or if the reversal will stop eventually and will anticipate a change when the charts show a lot of investor sentiment.

Combination with Other Analysis Methods

To make the most out of the technical analysis, you need to combine it with other charting methods on the market. You also need to use secondary data, such as sentiment analysis and indicators.

To achieve this, you need to go beyond pure technical analysis, and combine other market forecast methods in line with technical work. You can use technical analysis along with fundamental analysis to improve the performance of your portfolio.

You can also combine technical analysis with economics and quantitative analysis. For instance, you can use neural networks along with technical analysis to identify the relationships in the market. Other traders make use of technical analysis with astrology.

Other traders go for newspaper polls, sentiment indicators to come with deductions.

The Different Types of Charts Used in Technical Analysis

Candlestick Chart

This is a charting method that came from the Japanese. The method fills the interval between opening and closing prices to show a relationship. These candles use color-coding to show the closing points. You will come across black, red, white, blue, or green candles to represent the closing point at any time.

Open-High-Low-Close Chart (OHLC)

These are also referred to as bar charts, and they give you a connection between the maximum and minimum prices in a trading period. They usually feature a tick on the left side to show the open price and one on the right to show the closing price.

Line Chart

This is a chart that maps the closing price values using a line segment.

The Benefits of Technical Analysis in Options Trading

The benefits arise from the fact that traders are usually asking a lot of questions touching on the price of the market and entry points. While the forecast for prices is a huge task, the use of technical analysis makes it easier to handle.

The Major Advantages of Technical Analysis Include

Expert Trend Analysis

This is the biggest advantage of technical analysis in any market. With this method, you can predict the direction of the market at any time. You can determine whether the market will move up, down or sideways easily.

Entry and Exit Points

As a trader, you need to know when to place a trade and when to opt-out. The entry point is all about knowing the right time to enter the trade for good returns. Exiting a trade is also vital because it allows you to reduce losses.

Leverage Early Signals

Every trader looks for ways to get early signals to assist them in making decisions. Technical analysis gives you signals to trigger a decision on your part. This is usually ideal when you suspect that a trend will reverse soon. Remember the time the trend reverses are when you need to make crucial **decisions.**

It Is Quick

In options trading, you need to go with techniques that give you fast results. Additionally, getting technical analysis data is cheaper than other techniques in fundamental analysis, with some companies offering free charting programs.

You Understand Trends

If the prices on the market were to gyrate randomly without any direction, you would find it hard to make money. While these trends run in all directions, the prices always move in trends. Directional bias allows you to leverage the benefits of making money. Technical analysis allows you to determine when a trend occurs and when it doesn't occur, or when it is in reversal.

Many of the profitable techniques that are used by the traders to make money followed trends. This means that you find the right trend and then look for opportunities that allow you to enter the market in the same direction as the trend. This helps you to capitalize on the price movement.

Trends run in various degrees. The degree of the trend determines how much money you make, whether in the short term or long-term trading. Technical analysis gives you all the tools that make it possible for you to do this.

Technical analysis uses common patterns to give you the information to trade. However, you need to understand that history will not be exact when it repeats itself, though. The current analysis will be either bigger or smaller, depending on the existing market conditions. The only thing is that it won't be a replica of the prior pattern.

This pans out easily because most human psychology doesn't change so much, and you will see that the emotions have a hand in making sure that prices rise and fall. The emotions that traders exhibit create a lot of patterns that lead to changes in prices all the time. As a trader, you need to identify these patterns and then use them for trading. Use prior history to guide you and then the current price as a trigger of the trade.

Applicable Over a Wide Time Frame

When you learn technical analysis, you get to apply it to many areas in different markets, including options. All the trading in a market is based mostly on the patters that are a result of human behavior. These patterns can then be mapped out on a chart to be used across the markets.

While there is some difference between analyzing different securities, you will be able to use technical analysis in most of the markets.

Additionally, you can use the analysis in any timeframe, which is applicable whether you use hourly, daily, or weekly charts. These markets are usually taken to be fractal, which essentially means that patterns that appear on a small scale will also be present on a large scale as well.

Technical Indicators

Technical indicators come into play in options trading when you need to determine turning points for underlying stock and the trends that get them to this point. When used correctly, they can help to determine the optimal time to buy or sell and also predict movement cycles. In general, technical indicators are calculated based on the pricing pattern of the underlying stock. Relevant data includes highs and lows, opening price, volume and closing price. They typically take into account the data regarding a stock's price from the past few periods, based on the charts the person who is doing the analyzing prefers.

This information is then used to identify trends that show what has been happening regarding a specific stock and then using past information to determine likely results for the future. Technical indicators come in both leading and lagging varieties. Indicators that lag are based on data that already exists and make it easier to determine if a trend is in the process of forming or if the stock in question is simply trading within a range. The stronger the trend that the lagging indicator pinpoints, the greater the chance it is going to continue into the future. They typically drop the ball when it comes to predicting potential pullbacks or rally points, however.

Technical Analysis Secrets to Become the Best Trader

To make use of technical analysis the right way, you need to follow time-testing approaches that have made the technique a gold mine for many traders. Let us look at the various tips that will take you from novice to pro in just a few days:

Use More than One Indicator

Numbers make trading easy, but it also applies to the way you apply your techniques. For one, you need to know that just because one technical indicator is better than using one, applying a second indicator is better than using just one. The use of more than one indicator is one of the best ways to confirm a trend. It also increases the odds of being right.

As a trader, you will never be 100 percent right at all times, and you might even find that the odds are stashed against you when everything is plain to see. However, don't demand too much from your indicators such that you end up with analysis paralysis.

To achieve this, make use of indicators that complement each other rather than the ones that clash against each other.

Go for Multiple Time Frames

Using the same buy signal every day allows you to have confidence that the indicator is giving you all you need to know to trade. However, make sure you look for a way to use multiple timeframes to confirm a trend. When you have a doubt, it is wise that you increase the timeframe from an hour to a day or from a daily chart to a weekly chart.

CHAPTER 10

Steps by Step: Day Trading Business

Build a watch list

S ince there are so many stocks to trade, you can't possibly watch them all on a daily basis. Before you really get going, create a list of stocks whose movements you can monitor. It is best to choose one or two sectors then choose a few stocks from each to put on your watch list.

Some of the most popular sectors are:

- Banking
- Precious Metals
- Semiconductor
- Automotive
- Pharmaceuticals
- Retail
- Internet

Choose one or two sectors that you would like to follow then track the movement of the top issues. Limit the number of stocks that you follow to about 10 per sector, maxing out at 20 stocks being monitored at a time. This will allow you to truly track and understand their movement trends.

Choose stocks

It is advisable to trade on stocks that have a high enough volume that you can quickly enter and exit trades. Your brokerage account will likely provide a "most active" list, which will give you the top 10 or 20 highest volume stocks; that is a great place to start. Finding a screener that will go beyond this ranking, though, will be advantageous as it will allow you a broader list and possibly stocks that are not being tracked by every investor. It is also a good idea to look at stocks that are rising in high volume relative to themselves. If a stock usually trades 3 million shares per day, but today has 5 million shares traded by market open, this is certainly something worth exploring.

Entry and exit strategy

You need to know when to enter the market. Candlestick and bar patterns are ideal triggers to use.

Knowing the right market entry points is dependent on how well you research the market and the trading activity as a whole.

The best way of knowing when to enter could be determined by carefully monitoring how certain stocks perform. This means that you need to follow the market trends carefully. Based on historical data, you should find out whether the securities can drop to a specific price you think it would be best to buy.

Wait, it shouldn't just stop there. Besides knowing your entry points, you should also identify the ideal exit strategy. This is where you exit the trade without incurring huge losses. Exiting at the right time also guarantees you close the day with something to smile about. This applies to situations where you make profits from your trading process.

Certainly, with day trading, anything can go wrong. There are times when markets will quickly drop, which could affect your returns. Knowing when to exit is, therefore, important. Essentially, exiting is not just about selling when things don't go your way. You also need to exit when things are going as you expected. This ensures that you make the best out of your investment. You should always set your feelings aside as the market will not always be on your side. Know when to stop at the right times

Buy and sell

Buy

When it comes to buying stocks or securities, you must buy them in bulk. It is not possible to buy one or two stocks. There will be a minimum purchase amount that will be mentioned next to the stock value. Remember that you have to make a minimum investment when you buy stocks and this minimum will differ from company to company. It will also differ from website to website and so, you must look at the minimum amount that needs to be invested in order to buy stocks for day trading purposes. If you are choosing "options," then you will have to pay an advance towards the stocks or securities that you wish to reserve.

Sell

The next step is to sell all your stocks and securities. This is done by the end of the day. Selling is also known as liquidating and for options, it is known as liquidating your position. Remember that you have to sell your stock on the same day in order for it to be called day trading. If you hold on to your stock overnight, then it will be known as regular trading. Once you sell it, you will have a chance to make a profit. Your profit will be deducted from the value of the stock at the time of purchase and transferred to your account. But remember that you must invest wisely and make sure that you are coming into good profit before deciding to buy and sell stocks and securities. Look at the market

With the advent of online trading, this has made it possible to have a wide array of financial instruments that traders can depend on. In this case, individuals can trade on other financial instruments besides stocks, futures, and options. Recently, there have been other trading options, including the Foreign Exchange Market (forex), Single Stock Futures (SSF) and Exchange Traded Funds (ETFs).

It is worth pointing out that the existing financial securities have been improved to include electronic contracts of notable commodities such as natural gas, gold, silver, grains, and crude oil. These futures are getting popular each day amongst day traders. It is for this reason that pit-traded commodities have been overtaken by the high volume of mini and electronic contracts.

Essentially, the internet has made it possible to trade on anything. Take, for instance, real estate, it is possible to enter this industry without actually owning any properties. This is made possible through Real Estate Investment Trusts (REITs). To understand how you can select an appropriate market to trade, it is imperative to learn about the different markets individually. There are several markets which you could trade in. However, we'll focus on the most popular, including stocks, futures, forex, and stock options. These markets will be scrutinized based on capital requirements, leverage, liquidity, and   volatility.

Capital Requirements

Of course, one of the main considerations that most traders would bear in mind is the amount of capital that they require to initiate their trading activity. Therefore, it is worth examining the markets based on the amount of capital that you would require to begin day trading. Often, experienced traders will recommend the idea of starting small and growing gradually. This gives a novice trader ample time to learn and master the art of day trading.

Leverage

Another essential factor to mull over is leverage. After understanding how to trade on different markets, a trader could always make the best out of the little capital they are using to trade. In this case, leveraged markets give them the opportunity of maximizing their profits by simply using a small amount of capital. Consequently, the advantage gained in using leverage is that a small account can be developed quickly.

Liquidity

Understanding markets based on liquidity is essential. Focusing on liquid markets warrants that traders circumvent the common market issues of slippage and manipulation. Undeniably, any trader would want to make sure that they receive accurate fills for their orders.

Volatility

Without volatility, it would be impossible to make money from different markets. Therefore, markets have to be moving for people to make money. In relation to this, understanding the most volatile market guarantees that a trader puts their money in viable markets.

By now you must be curious to know how markets vary. The following paragraphs will discuss basic information about the different markets you could turn to out there. Undeniably, knowledge is power. Hence, knowing what to expect from these markets is important for any trader.

Proceed

As a novice trader, you need to test the waters a bit. Remember, people make and lose money day trading. It's unrealistic for you to expect every move you make to be profitable. This means you should avoid taking on too much risk as well as not risking too much of your investment capital all at once. While testing your trading approach against the market before putting up money is a good idea, keep your initial investments manageable until you gain experience and confidence in your approach. You'll find that things feel different when you actually have money on the line. Beginning day traders should try to understand and manage their reactions to market movements. Make a plan before investing, set entry and departure targets, as well as a target to bail on a stock that's moving in the wrong direction.

CHAPTER 11

How to Determine your Goals for

Trading

D ay by day objectives is, to a great extent, controlled by your degree of hazard resistance. For example, you chance 1% per exchange. My day by day benefit cutoff is 2%, so you just need a couple of effective exchanges without any misfortunes to hit that mark.

If you are just gambling 5% per exchange, a progressively practical everyday benefit cutoff maybe 1% every day. It is going for 2%, while gambling .5% and would take two to four fruitful exchanges without any misfortunes to accomplish. At the end of the day, it's not prone to occur.

Note: Don't simply hop into the market. Gain proficiency with a decent trading framework, and afterward backtest and demo exchange until you demonstrate to yourself that you can be reliable over the long haul (months or years – not days or weeks).

At the point when you begin trading a live record, utilize the littlest part size (or the number of offers, contracts, and so forth…) accessible to you from the start. Step by step, increment your presentation per exchange to your ideal hazard level as you become acquainted with the mental obstacles of trading genuine money.

Best traders would prescribe utilizing .5 – 1% per exchange. Extremely propelled traders regularly hazard 3% or more per exchange. What amount of money would you say you will lose per exchange? When you have decided your own degree of hazard resistance, you can decide a day by day objective or cutoff.

Week by Week and Monthly Goals

From that point, your week after week and month to month shorts can be set. I have a progressively forceful hazard resilience, so I may benefit cutoff targets are as per the following: 2% every day, 5% week after week, and 15% month to month. I don't utilize yearly shorts.

These objectives may appear to be high to certain traders, yet they are sensible for me.

Note: This doesn't imply that you make 2% consistently, 5% consistently, and so on.... In the event that you make 2% in a day, that is a decent day of trading. Moreover, 5% is a decent seven day stretch of trading.

If you are not reliable yet, you should concentrate on learning a beneficial trading framework and turning into a long haul, reliably productive trader. In case you're simply beginning, going for 5% every month bodes well.

If you feel that you can twofold your record at regular intervals in trading, you are not prone to set reasonable benefit targets. You will probably overtrade your way to a littler record balance.

You will chance excessively, and you will lose excessively. Ravenousness makes traders be careless and overactive in the market, which prompts botches. Little predictable and exacerbated benefits will prompt a fortune over the long haul.

Keep in mind: Money management shorts work the two different ways. In the event that you are down 2% in one day (or two misfortunes straight), Stop trading that day. Quit trading in the event that you lose 3% in a multi-week. In conclusion, Use 5% as my month to month misfortunes cutoff. Remember that you will have a progressively forceful hazard resistance.

www.ingramcontent.com/pod-product-compliance
Lightning Source LLC
Chambersburg PA
CBHW071722210326
41597CB00017B/2562